My name is

· and ·

MY FAVORITE COLOR IS ORANGE

ILLUSTRATED BY **MARIA NERADOVA**

odd
dot

New York

An imprint of Macmillan Children's Publishing Group, LLC
120 Broadway, New York, NY 10271 • OddDot.com

ILLUSTRATOR   **Maria Neradova**
DESIGNER   **Abby Dening**
EDITOR   **Daniel Nayeri**
ART DIRECTOR   **Timothy Hall**
CREATIVE DIRECTOR   **Christina Quintero**
PRODUCTION EDITOR   **Kathy Wielgosz**
MANAGING EDITOR   **Jennifer Healey**
PRODUCTION MANAGER   **Barbara Cho**

ISBN 978-1-250-76837-7

First edition, 2021
Printed in China by Hung Hing Off-set Printing Co. Ltd.,
Heshan City, Guangdong Province

1 3 5 7 9 10 8 6 4 2

Joyful Books for Curious Minds

NAME THAT ORANGE

There are so many shades of orange in the world that some of them don't even have names yet. What would you name these?

WHY ORANGE?

Orange is the greatest color in the world because . . .

But I also love it because . . .

Whenever I see orange, I feel . . .

When I'm sad, orange makes me . . .

When I'm happy, orange makes me . . .

_____ looks better when it's orange.

_____ tastes better when it's orange.

_____ should be orange.

GOLDEN GATE BRIDGE IN CALIFORNIA, USA

HOUSE OF ORANGE-NASSAU IN THE NETHERLANDS

THE ORANGE CITY, YAZD, IRAN

MARIGOLDS IN MEXICO

BENGAL TIGERS IN INDIA

ORANGE ROUGHY FISH IN NEW ZEALAND

COLOR YOUR BIG, ORANGE WORLD

WHAT'S THE DIFFERENCE?

There are twelve differences between these two pictures.
Can you spot them all?

FIND THAT ORANGE

Go on an orange scavenger hunt! Can you find these shades of orange in real life? Now draw pictures of the things you found!

ORANGE-A-LICIOUS TREATS

ORANGE SPRITZER

INGREDIENTS

2 cups fresh-squeezed orange juice
(from about 6 oranges)

2 cups sparkling water

orange slices

DIRECTIONS

1. Stir orange juice and sparkling water together in a large pitcher.

2. To serve, pour over ice and garnish with orange slices.

3. Enjoy!

ORANGE CREAM MILKSHAKE

INGREDIENTS

grated zest of 4 oranges
(add more for stronger
orange taste!)

2 teaspoons orange extract

1 cup milk

1 pint vanilla ice cream

orange slices

SPECIAL EQUIPMENT

blender

DIRECTIONS

1. Place first four ingredients in blender and blend until smooth.

2. To serve, pour into glasses and garnish with orange slices.

3. Enjoy!

DYEING FOR ORANGE

Did you know that the stuff you have around the house can dye an egg your favorite color? It's true! With these ingredients, you can turn your eggs orange in no time!

YOU WILL NEED

- 8 tablespoons paprika powder
- 4 cups water
- a pot with a lid
- 4 tablespoons white vinegar
- a dozen hard-boiled white eggs
- a bowl or dish big enough to hold dye and eggs in a single layer
- tongs or slotted spoon
- egg carton

DIRECTIONS

1. Bring paprika powder and water to a boil in pot.

2. Reduce heat to low and simmer, covered, for 15 to 30 minutes, until dye is a few shades darker than the color you want.

3. Remove from heat and let dye cool to room temperature. (This takes 2–3 hours.)

4. Stir vinegar into cooled dye.

5. Place eggs in bowl in a single layer and carefully pour dye over them. Make sure eggs are completely submerged.

6. Let eggs sit in dye overnight, covered, in the fridge.

7. Remove eggs from dye with tongs or slotted spoon and set them in carton to dry.

HIDDEN ORANGE

Pumpkins aren't the only thing you'll find in this pumpkin patch.
Can you spot the ten things hiding here?

ORANGE DREAMS

If I could **HAVE** any orange thing, it would be . . .

If I could **EAT** any orange thing, it would be . . .

If I could turn **ANYTHING** orange, it would be . . .

If I could **SEE** any orange thing, it would be . . .

If I could turn **ANYONE** orange it would be . . .

If it were up to **ME**,

would all be orange.

MY PERFECT ORANGE OUTFIT

Draw your perfect orange outfit.

LUCKY PAPER STARS!

Use the paper strips on the right and follow the instructions to fold a skyful of lucky orange stars!

Start with a strip of paper approximately 11 inches long and ½ inch wide. Make a loose loop near one end of the strip.

Tie the loop into a knot and tighten gently so it makes a pentagonal (five-sided) shape.

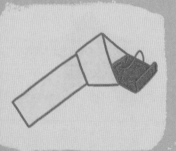 

Tuck the short end into the pentagon. Then wrap the long end around the edge of the pentagon.

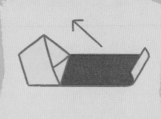

Continue turning and wrapping the long end around the pentagon. Don't press too hard.

Repeat until you reach the end of the strip.

Trim any excess if necessary, then tuck the remaining length of strip into the pentagon.

Gently squish the sides of the pentagon to create creases between the five points using your finger nails. You now have a lucky paper star!

MUSEUM OF ORANGE

The paintings in the Orange Hall of Fame have been stolen! Can you re-create them?

The Meanest Goldfish

The Scariest Jack-o'-Lantern

The Cutest Carrot

The Silliest Orange

The World's First Basketball-Playing Tiger

DRAW IT ORANGE

Follow the instructions to learn how to draw each orange object or animal.

FOX

1   2   3

MONARCH
BUTTERFLY

1   2   3   4   5

DAYLILY

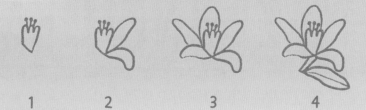

1   2   3   4

RED-SPOTTED
NEWT

1   2   3

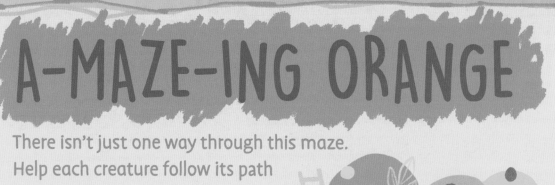

A-MAZE-ING ORANGE

There isn't just one way through this maze.
Help each creature follow its path
to the other side!

THE FACTS ABOUT ORANGE

CARROTS WEREN'T ALWAYS ORANGE!

They were yellow or purple until the 1600s, when Dutch horticulturalists bred the orange vegetable we know and love today.

NOT ALL ORANGES ARE ORANGE!
In Thailand, oranges are green on the outside and orange on the inside.

BASKETBALLS WERE NOT ALWAYS ORANGE!
They were first made of a dark brown material that made them difficult to see on the court. By 1957, Spalding Company developed a new, orange-colored basketball that's been used ever since!

The **WORD ORANGE** comes from Arabic *nāranj*, Persian *nārang*, and Sanskrit *nāraṅga* for orange tree.

SPICES LIKE SAFFRON AND TURMERIC
are often used to dye cloth and other items in orange hues.

WHEN ASTRONAUTS on American spacecraft lift off for outer space and come back to Earth, they wear orange space suits so that rescuers can easily see them if necessary.

MEDITATION ON ORANGE!

Color this design with every shade of orange you can find—then write your name in the center.

WHERE'S THAT ORANGE?

Can you find these particular shades of orange? Draw a line from each shade to where you see it in the picture.

TURN IT ORANGE

Pretty much everything should be orange, right? What in the world would you like to turn orange? Draw it here.

THE ART OF ORANGE

Complete the crosshatching to create your own three-dimensional tiger!

ONE LINE

TWO LINES

THREE LINES

FOUR LINES

PAINT BY ORANGE

What color are these goldfish?
Fill in the key at the bottom with
your favorite shades of orange.
Then color-by-number!

1 2 3 4 5 6 7

A LOVE LETTER IN ORANGE

Let people know how much you love them—and orange! Cut out and fold this card and envelope, then write your message inside and send it to someone special.

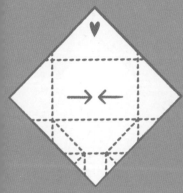

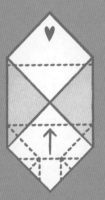

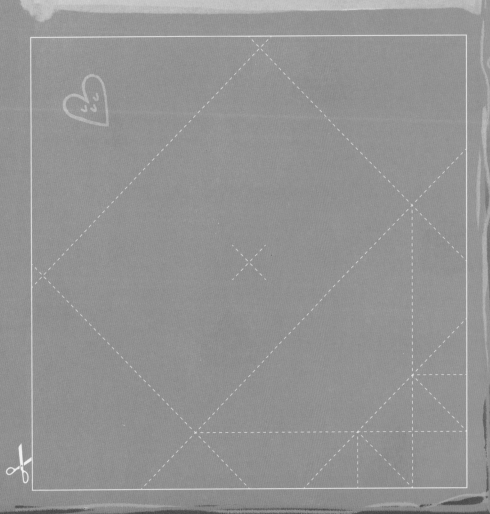

I LOVE YOU...
AS MUCH AS
I LOVE
ORANGE!

SEEING DOUBLE

These orangutans may all look the same, but only two are identical. Can you find them?

ORANGE CITY

Paint this town orange! Add your own buildings to the skyline. Build on the samples you see here, or use your own imagination.

CONNECT THE ORANGE

Connect the dots with an orange marker or crayon to reveal this orange creature.

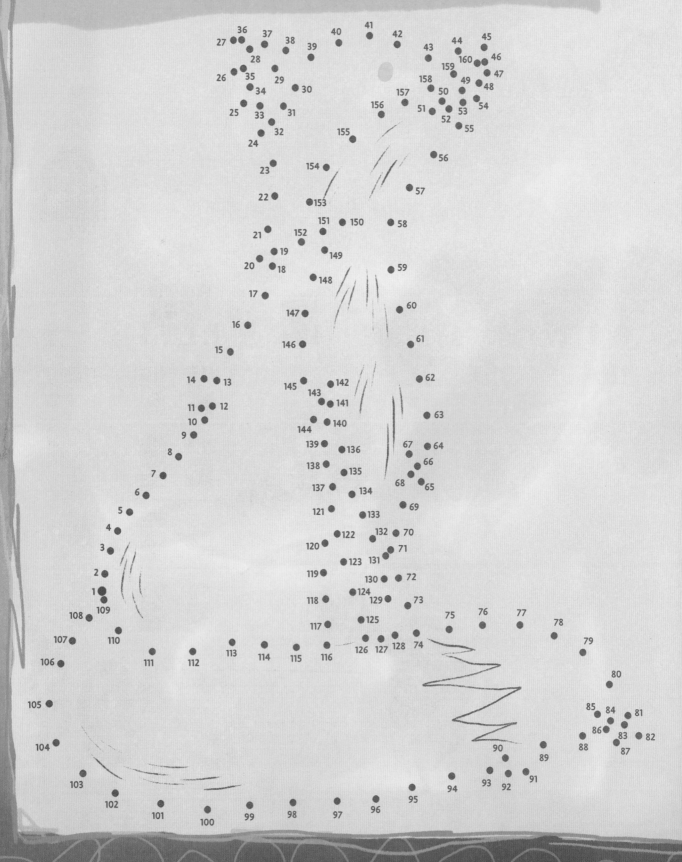

MY FAVORITE ORANGES

My favorite orange thing
IN THE WORLD is . . .

My favorite orange thing
I OWN is . . .

My favorite orange PLACE is . . .

My favorite orange FOOD is . . .

My favorite piece of orange CLOTHING is . . .

My favorite orange
ANIMAL is . . .

My favorite orange DRINK is . . .

My favorite SHADE of orange is . . .

My SECOND-FAVORITE SHADE of orange is . . .

ORANGE PAIRINGS

What are your favorite colors to pai
with orange? Pick different colors to
finish each picture and discover you
favorite orange color combination!

DO YOU WANT TO COME TO MY PARTY?

Throw a party with all orange things! Cut out and fold these invitations, fill in the details, and send!

YOU'RE INVITED TO CELEBRATE MY FAVORITE COLOR, **ORANGE!**

Time:
Date:
Place:
Your friend,

YOU'RE INVITED TO CELEBRATE MY FAVORITE COLOR, **ORANGE!**

Time:
Date:
Place:
Your friend,

YOU'RE INVITED TO CELEBRATE MY FAVORITE COLOR, **ORANGE!**

Time:
Date:
Place:
Your friend,

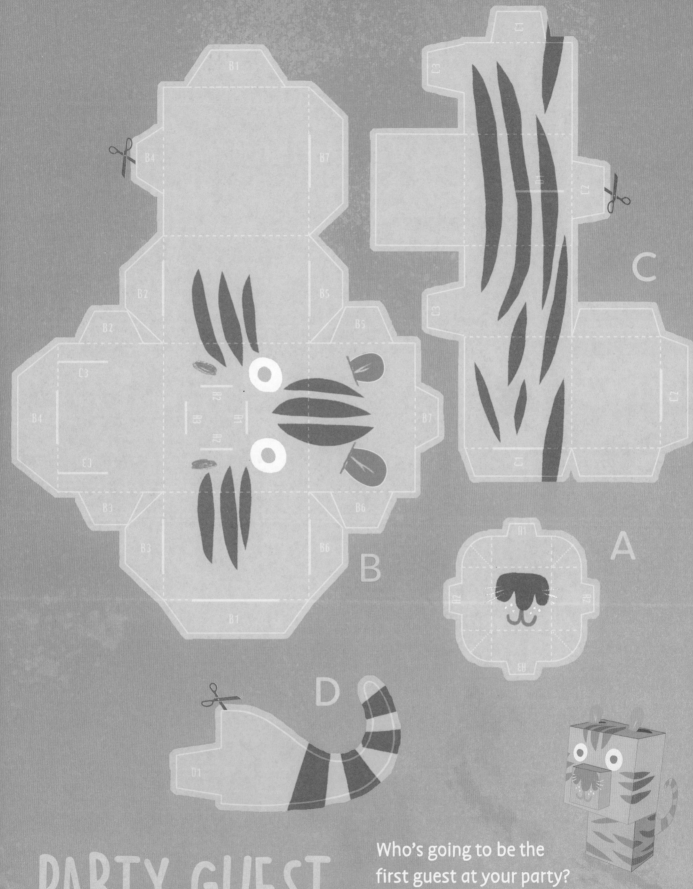

PARTY GUEST

*Learn how to assemble your party guest on the next page.

Who's going to be the first guest at your party? They'd better be wearing orange! Follow the instructions to create a party guest who can help you welcome everyone else!

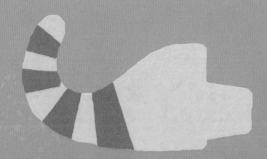

HOW TO ASSEMBLE
YOUR PARTY GUEST

Cut out pieces along the solid lines.
Fold along the dotted lines.

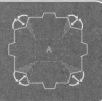

Fold piece A by folding in the corners to bring edges together.

Assemble by matching up tabs and slots (tab A1 inserts into slot A1). Start by attaching piece A to B, then piece C into the C1 and C2 slots on piece B.

Optional: Partially cut the ears and fold them out.

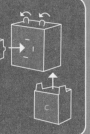

Insert piece D into the D1 slot on piece C.